WALLINGFORD PUBLIC LIBRARY
WALLINGFORD, CONNECTICUT 06492

IT'S SCIENCE!

Full of Energy

Sally Hewitt

WALLINGFORD PUBLIC LIBRARY
WALLINGFORD, CONNECTICUT 06492

CHILDREN'S PRESS®

A Division of Grolier Publishing

NEW YORK • LONDON • HONG KONG • SYDNEY
DANBURY, CONNECTICUT

J531.6
HEW

© Franklin Watts 1997
First American edition 1998 by
Children's Press, A Division of Grolier Publishing
Sherman Turnpike, Danbury, CT 06816

Hewitt, Sally.
    Full of energy / Sally Hewitt
        p. cm. -- (It's science!)
    Includes index.
    Summary: An interactive approach introducing the concept of energy
as found in food, sun, wind, water, and other sources and as used
for nutrition, warmth, and motion.
    Spine title: It's science!
    ISBN 0-516-20792-x
    1. Force and energy--Juvenile literature. 2. Energy metabolism-
-Juvenile literature. [1. Force and energy. 2. Metabolism.]
I. Title. II. Title: It's science! III. Series: Hewitt, Sally.
It's science!
QC73.4.H53 1997
531'.6--DC21   97-3550
                                                                       CIP
                                                                       AC

Series editor: Rachel Cooke
Art director: Robert Walster
Designer: Mo Choy
Picture research: Sarah Snashall
Consultant: Sally Nankivell-Aston
Photography: Ray Moller unless otherwise acknowledged

Printed in Malaysia

Photographic acknowledgments:
Bruce Coleman pp. 10 bottom (Geoff Dore), 12 (Hans Reinhard)
Robert Harding pp. 13 bottom left (Fukuhara Inc.), 18 top (Adam Woolfit),
25 bottom (Ian Griffiths), 26 top (Nigel Francis), 27 bottom (Philip Craven)
Oxford Scientific Films p. 11 bottom (Doug Allan)
NHPA pp 10 top (Stephen Krasemann), 11 top (Stephen Dalton), 13 bottom center (Robert Erwin)
Zefa p. 23 left.
The publishers would also like to thank the following for their help with items in this book:
Tridias, 6 Bennett Street, Bath BA1 2QP 01225 314730 pp. 17, 24. Thank you, too, to our models:
Zara Bilgrami, Ken King, Camilla Knipe, Wilfred Cross, Stephan Lee, Lauren Shoota, Jordan
Hardley and Henry Moller.

Contents

Working Hard

Justin is full of **energy**! He needs energy to **work** hard. Did you know that you are full of energy, too?

Even when you are asleep, you use energy. You are breathing, your heart is beating, and you might even be dreaming.

You use energy for everything you do.

Sometimes you don't use very much energy, and sometimes you use a lot.

TRY IT OUT!

Try doing these
three things:
★ reading
★ walking
★ skipping

Can you tell which one uses up the most energy?
Which one can you do for the longest amount of time?
Which one makes you tired the fastest?

7

Feeling Hungry

Food gives you energy. When you feel hungry, your body is reminding you that you need to eat.

Young children use lots of energy. They are growing fast, and they are always on the move so they need plenty of food.

 **LOOK AGAIN**

Look again at pages 6 and 7.
What might you do that uses up lots of energy and would make you feel hungry?

Some kinds of food give you more energy than others.
A cheese and salad sandwich is packed
with energy. Bananas and potatoes
give you quite a lot of energy.

If you eat too little, you soon get weak.
If you eat more food than you need,
you will put on weight.

Some food contains things that are good
for you as well as energy. You need to eat
a good mixture of foods to stay healthy.

 TRY IT OUT!

Make a list of all the things
you have eaten today.
Which food do you think
gave you the most energy?

9

Animal Energy

It is not just people who eat for energy. All animals need food to live.

Lions eat meat to give them energy. There is a lot of energy in meat. Lions don't need to eat every day.

Deer have to munch leaves and grass nearly all day to get enough food to give them the energy they need.

Food gives animals energy to keep warm. But some animals, such as lizards and snakes, need to warm themselves in the sun as well.

Seals get the energy to keep warm from the fish they eat.
They also have an extra layer of fat to keep their bodies warm, as they swim in icy cold water.

 THINK ABOUT IT!

In the winter, some animals cannot find enough food. To save energy, they curl up and sleep until spring. This long sleep is called **hibernation**.

What do you do to keep warm?

Plant Energy

Plants, like this tree, don't have to hunt or look for food. They can make their own!

Plants get energy from sunlight and turn it into food in their green leaves.

Plants store the food they need to grow in bulbs, seeds, and roots.

👁 LOOK AGAIN

What can you see on this page that is good for you to eat?

Tulip bulb   Bean   Carrot

People and animals cannot make their own food. They have to eat to get their energy.

All this food comes from plants and is full of energy from the sun.

The sun gives out energy.

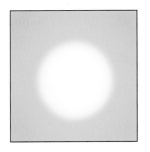

Plants use energy from the sun to grow.

You eat the plant.

Now *you* are full of energy from the sun!

Full of Energy

Coal in a bucket, **batteries**, food, and gasoline in a pump don't look as though they can do much.

In fact all these things can help us. They are full of energy that can be used to make things work.

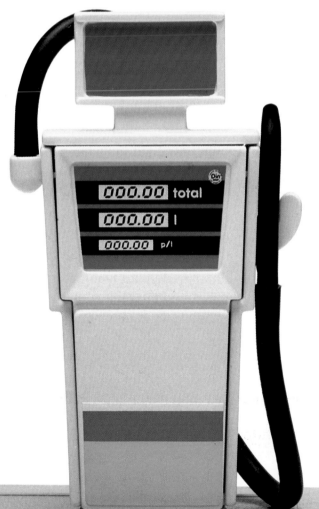

👁 LOOK AGAIN

Look again at page 12. What is full of the energy this tulip needs to grow?

14

What **fuel** can you see on the opposite page that is full of the energy this car needs to go?

What gives a person energy to play soccer?

What gives a flashlight energy to shine?

What fuel gives a fire energy to keep you warm?

 TRY IT OUT!

On a warm, sunny day, put a brick outside and let the sun shine on it for a few hours.
Take the brick inside and feel with your hands how warm it is. The brick has stored up heat.
It is full of **stored energy** from the sun.

Changing Energy

Did you know that you can use the energy in your body
to make different kinds of energy?
Heat, **sound**, and **movement** are different kinds of energy.

 TRY IT OUT!

HEAT

Rub your hands
together as quickly
as you can. You have
used your energy to
make heat.

MOVEMENT

Push a book with your
hands and watch it
move. You have used
your energy to move
your arms and hands
– and move the book!

SOUND
Say "hello" and hear
your voice. You have
used your energy to
make sound.

Clay, a toy duck, and drumsticks cannot do anything by themselves. But you can give them the energy they need to get warm, to move, and to make a noise.

TRY IT OUT!

Roll the clay hard on a table top to make it warm.

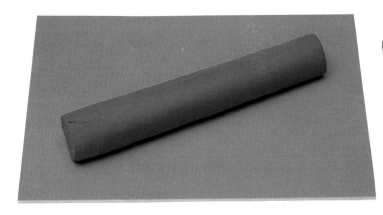

Pull the toy along to make it move.

Beat a drum with the drum sticks to make a noise.

LOOK AGAIN

Look at all the things you have done on these pages. How did you make heat? How did you make sound? How did you make movement?

17

Electricity

Electricity is a special kind of energy that we use to make lights shine and make machines work.

Natural gas, oil, or coal is burned in power stations.

The heat energy this makes is changed into electricity.

The electricity flows through **cables** into our homes.

When we turn on a **switch**, the electricity flows through the wires in the light or machine and makes it work.

⚡ SAFETY WARNING

Never touch or play with the electrical outlets in the walls.

This battery stores electric current. Electricity from the battery flows along the metal inside the wire to the light bulb.

To make the light bulb glow, electricity must flow round a **circuit** back to the battery. A circuit is a complete circle.

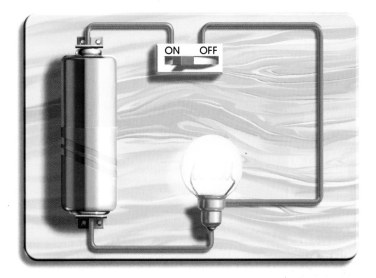

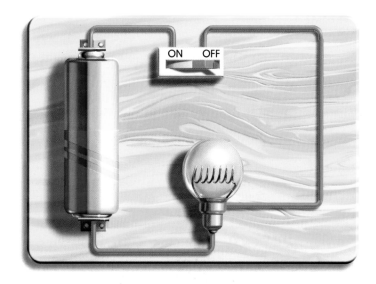

When the switch is turned on, the circuit is joined and the light comes on.

When the switch is turned off, the circuit is broken and the light goes out.

 TRY IT OUT!

Look inside a flashlight.
Can you see how the batteries touch a piece of metal at either end?
How do you think the switch turns the flashlight on and off?

Switch It On

Each one of these machines uses electricity to work. They all need to be switched on.

Which ones need to be plugged in to an electrical outlet? Which ones use batteries?

 **LOOK AGAIN**

Look again at page 19. Find something else that needs a battery to work.

What job does each of these machines do when it is switched on?

💡 THINK ABOUT IT!

Would any of these things be useful without electricity to make it work?

21

Keeping Warm

The girl, the pizza, and the room are all nice and warm. Heat energy has warmed each of them up.

If the girl moves out of the sun, if someone leaves the door of the room open, or if the pizza is left on the table, each will soon cool down.

💡 THINK ABOUT IT!

What can you do to stay cool on a warm day?

Heat energy from fireplaces and radiators can warm up a house.

Closing the curtains and keeping doors shut are two ways to keep the warm air in and the cold air out.

Clothes help to keep you warm.

What else can you do to keep a house warm?

Food can be covered and put on a hot plate to stay warm.

 LOOK AGAIN

Look again at page 11.
How do lizards and seals keep warm?

Moving Along

One quick burst of energy can make a ball, a jack-in-a-box, and a sled move, but they only keep moving for a short time.

The jack-in-a-box leaps into the air when you press down its spring and then let it go.

The ball moves when you throw or kick it.

The sled slides along when you give it a hard push.

24

Bicycles, trains, and cars keep moving for a long distance. They need to take their supply of energy with them.

You have to keep pedaling to move a bicycle along.

Electricity from an electric rail keeps the train moving.

LOOK AGAIN

Look again at page 14 to find what a car carries inside it to give it the energy to keep going.

Sun, Wind, and Water

The sun gives out huge amounts of energy in the form of heat. This is called solar energy.

Solar energy can be collected in **solar panels** and used to heat water. This house has solar panels on the roof.

 LOOK AGAIN

Look again at page 15.
What can store solar energy?

There is a lot of energy in running water.

Fast flowing water turns this water wheel round.
Inside the mill, the water wheel drives machinery that grinds corn.

THINK ABOUT IT!

Energy from the sun, moving water and the wind can be used to make electricity. Will this kind of energy ever run out?

There is energy in the wind too. It blows the sails of this wind mill round to pump water up from under the ground.

Sailors have used energy from the wind to sail their boats across the ocean for thousands of years.

 TRY IT OUT!

Make a sailing boat from:
– a food tray
– a long straw
– some colored paper
– a lump of clay
– sticky tape

Copy this model sailing boat. Blow into the sail and watch it move over your bath water. What else can you think of that you can move by blowing?

27

Useful Words

Battery A battery stores electric current. Batteries can be put into small electrical machines such as flashlights or tape recorders to give them the energy they need to work.

Cable A cable is a long line of wires wrapped in thick plastic. Electricity flows along the wires from power stations into our homes.

Circuit Electricity has to flow around an unbroken circle of wire. This circle is called a circuit.

Coal Coal was formed from plants that died millions of years ago. It is dug up from deep under the ground and burned for heat.

Electricity Electricity is a kind of energy that can be used to make things work.

Energy Energy is what people, animals, and machines need to give them the power to do work.

Heat energy When the sun shines or coal burns, heat energy is produced.

Movement energy When you push a book and make it move, you give the book movement energy.

Sound energy Sound is a kind of energy we hear with our ears.

Solar energy Energy from the sun is called solar energy.

Stored energy Energy is stored in things such as coal, batteries, and food. Coal must be burned, batteries must be turned on, and food must be eaten to release the energy.

Food People, animals, and plants all need food. They turn it into the energy they need to live and grow.

Fuel Coal, gas, and oil are all kinds of fuel. They can be burned to make energy.

Hibernation Some animals sleep all winter to save energy. This long sleep is called hibernation.

Natural gas The air all around us is a mixture of gases. Natural gas in another kind of gas that is burned as fuel. It is collected from under the ground, where it has been trapped for millions of years.

Solar panels Solar panels collect heat from the sun. This heat can then be used to warm up water.

Switch When you turn a switch off, it breaks an electrical circuit and cuts off electricity. When you turn a switch on, it joins the circuit up again so electricity can flow.

Work Work is done when something is moved or stopped. People and machines can both do work.

Index

About This Book

Children are natural scientists. They learn by touching and feeling, noticing, asking questions, and trying things out for themselves. The books in the *It's Science!* series are designed for the way children learn. Familiar objects are used as starting points for further learning. *Full of Energy* starts with a running child and explores energy.

Each double page spread introduces a new topic, such as electricity. Information is given, questions asked, and activities suggested that encourage children to make discoveries and develop new ideas for themselves.
Look out for these panels throughout the book:

TRY IT OUT! indicates a simple activity, using safe materials, that proves or explores a point.
THINK ABOUT IT! indicates a question inspired by the information on the page but that points the reader to areas not covered by the book.
LOOK AGAIN introduces a cross-referencing activity that links themes and facts through the book.

Encourage children not to take the familiar world for granted. Point things out, ask questions, and enjoy making scientific discoveries together.

j531.6   Hewitt, Sally.
HEW
         Full of energy.

Wallingford Public Library
Wallingford, CT 06492

A2170 403591 3

CHILDREN'S LIBRARY

WALLINGFORD PUBLIC LIBRARY
200 NO MAIN ST
WALLINGFORD CT   06492

BAKER & TAYLOR